Hello God!
Its Me Again

Today I Learned ...

Today I'm Grateful For ...

My Prayers Today ...

Amen!

Hello God!
Its Me Again

Today I Learned ...

Today I'm Grateful For ...

My Prayers Today ...

Amen!

Hello God!
Its Me Again

Today I Learned ...

Today I'm Grateful For ...

My Prayers Today ...

Amen!

Hello God!
Its Me Again

Today I Learned ...

Today I'm Grateful For ...

My Prayers Today ...

Amen!

Hello God!
Its Me Again

Today I Learned ...

Today I'm Grateful For ...

My Prayers Today ...

Amen!

Hello God!
Its Me Again

Today I Learned ...

Today I'm Grateful For ...

My Prayers Today ...

Amen!

Hello God!
Its Me Again

Today I Learned ...

Today I'm Grateful For ...

My Prayers Today ...

Amen!

Hello God!
Its Me Again

Today I Learned ...

Today I'm Grateful For ...

My Prayers Today ...

Amen!

Hello God!
Its Me Again

Today I Learned ...

Today I'm Grateful For ...

My Prayers Today ...

Amen!

Hello God!
Its Me Again

Today I Learned ...

Today I'm Grateful For ...

My Prayers Today ...

Amen!

Hello God!
Its Me Again

Today I Learned ...

Today I'm Grateful For ...

My Prayers Today ...

Amen!

Hello God!
Its Me Again

Today I Learned ...

Today I'm Grateful For ...

My Prayers Today ...

Amen!

Hello God!
Its Me Again

Today I Learned ...

Today I'm Grateful For ...

My Prayers Today ...

Amen!

Hello God!
Its Me Again

Today I Learned ...

Today I'm Grateful For ...

My Prayers Today ...

Amen!

Hello God!
Its Me Again

Today I Learned ...

Today I'm Grateful For ...

My Prayers Today ...

Amen!

Hello God!
Its Me Again

Today I Learned ...

Today I'm Grateful For ...

My Prayers Today ...

Amen!

Hello God!
Its Me Again

Today I Learned ...

Today I'm Grateful For ...

My Prayers Today ...

Amen!

Hello God!
Its Me Again

Today I Learned ...

Today I'm Grateful For ...

My Prayers Today ...

Amen!

Hello God!
Its Me Again

Today I Learned ...

Today I'm Grateful For ...

My Prayers Today ...

Amen!

Hello God!
Its Me Again

Today I Learned ...

Today I'm Grateful For ...

My Prayers Today ...

Amen!

Hello God!
Its Me Again

Today I Learned ...

Today I'm Grateful For ...

My Prayers Today ...

Amen!

Hello God!
Its Me Again

Today I Learned ...

Today I'm Grateful For ...

My Prayers Today ...

Amen!

Hello God!
Its Me Again

Today I Learned ...

Today I'm Grateful For ...

My Prayers Today ...

Amen!

Hello God!
Its Me Again

Today I Learned ...

Today I'm Grateful For ...

My Prayers Today ...

Amen!

Hello God!
Its Me Again

Today I Learned ...

Today I'm Grateful For ...

My Prayers Today ...

Amen!

Hello God!
Its Me Again

Today I Learned ...

Today I'm Grateful For ...

My Prayers Today ...

Amen!

Hello God!
Its Me Again

Today I Learned ...

Today I'm Grateful For ...

My Prayers Today ...

Amen!

Hello God!
Its Me Again

Today I Learned ...

Today I'm Grateful For ...

My Prayers Today ...

Amen!

Hello God!
Its Me Again

Today I Learned ...

Today I'm Grateful For ...

My Prayers Today ...

Amen!

Hello God!
Its Me Again

Today I Learned ...

Today I'm Grateful For ...

My Prayers Today ...

Amen!

Hello God!
Its Me Again

Today I Learned ...

Today I'm Grateful For ...

My Prayers Today ...

Amen!

Hello God!
Its Me Again

Today I Learned ...

Today I'm Grateful For ...

My Prayers Today ...

Amen!

Hello God!
Its Me Again

Today I Learned ...

Today I'm Grateful For ...

My Prayers Today ...

Amen!

Hello God!
Its Me Again

Today I Learned ...

Today I'm Grateful For ...

My Prayers Today ...

Amen!

Hello God!
Its Me Again

Today I Learned ...

Today I'm Grateful For ...

My Prayers Today ...

Amen!

Hello God!
Its Me Again

Today I Learned ...

Today I'm Grateful For ...

My Prayers Today ...

Amen!

Hello God!
Its Me Again

Today I Learned ...

Today I'm Grateful For ...

My Prayers Today ...

Amen!

Hello God!
Its Me Again

Today I Learned ...

Today I'm Grateful For ...

My Prayers Today ...

Amen!

Hello God!
Its Me Again

Today I Learned ...

Today I'm Grateful For ...

My Prayers Today ...

Amen!

Hello God!
Its Me Again

Today I Learned ...

Today I'm Grateful For ...

My Prayers Today ...

Amen!

Hello God!
Its Me Again

Today I Learned ...

Today I'm Grateful For ...

My Prayers Today ...

Amen!

Hello God!
Its Me Again

Today I Learned ...

Today I'm Grateful For ...

My Prayers Today ...

Amen!

Hello God!
Its Me Again

Today I Learned ...

Today I'm Grateful For ...

My Prayers Today ...

Amen!

Hello God!
Its Me Again

Today I Learned ...

Today I'm Grateful For ...

My Prayers Today ...

Amen!

Hello God!
Its Me Again

Today I Learned ...

Today I'm Grateful For ...

My Prayers Today ...

Amen!

Hello God!
Its Me Again

Today I Learned ...

Today I'm Grateful For ...

My Prayers Today ...

Amen!

Hello God!
Its Me Again

Today I Learned ...

Today I'm Grateful For ...

My Prayers Today ...

Amen!

Hello God!
Its Me Again

Today I Learned ...

Today I'm Grateful For ...

My Prayers Today ...

Amen!

Hello God!
Its Me Again

Today I Learned ...

Today I'm Grateful For ...

My Prayers Today ...

Amen!

Hello God!
Its Me Again

Today I Learned ...

Today I'm Grateful For ...

My Prayers Today ...

Amen!

Hello God!
Its Me Again

Today I Learned ...

Today I'm Grateful For ...

My Prayers Today ...

Amen!

Hello God!
Its Me Again

Today I Learned ...

Today I'm Grateful For ...

My Prayers Today ...

Amen!

Hello God!
Its Me Again

Today I Learned ...

Today I'm Grateful For ...

My Prayers Today ...

Amen!

Hello God!
Its Me Again

Today I Learned ...

Today I'm Grateful For ...

My Prayers Today ...

Amen!

Hello God!
Its Me Again

Today I Learned ...

Today I'm Grateful For ...

My Prayers Today ...

Amen!

Hello God!
Its Me Again

Today I Learned ...

Today I'm Grateful For ...

My Prayers Today ...

Amen!

Hello God!
Its Me Again

Today I Learned ...

Today I'm Grateful For ...

My Prayers Today ...

Amen!

Hello God!
Its Me Again

Today I Learned ...

Today I'm Grateful For ...

My Prayers Today ...

Amen!

Hello God!
Its Me Again

Today I Learned ...

Today I'm Grateful For ...

My Prayers Today ...

Amen!

Hello God!
Its Me Again

Today I Learned ...

Today I'm Grateful For ...

My Prayers Today ...

Amen!

Hello God!
Its Me Again

Today I Learned ...

Today I'm Grateful For ...

My Prayers Today ...

Amen!

Hello God!
Its Me Again

Today I Learned ...

Today I'm Grateful For ...

My Prayers Today ...

Amen!

Hello God!
Its Me Again

Today I Learned ...

Today I'm Grateful For ...

My Prayers Today ...

Amen!

Hello God!
Its Me Again

Today I Learned ...

Today I'm Grateful For ...

My Prayers Today ...

Amen!

Hello God!
Its Me Again

Today I Learned ...

Today I'm Grateful For ...

My Prayers Today ...

Amen!

Hello God!
Its Me Again

Today I Learned ...

Today I'm Grateful For ...

My Prayers Today ...

Amen!

Hello God!
Its Me Again

Today I Learned ...

Today I'm Grateful For ...

My Prayers Today ...

Amen!

Hello God!
Its Me Again

Today I Learned ...

Today I'm Grateful For ...

My Prayers Today ...

Amen!

Hello God!
Its Me Again

Today I Learned ...

Today I'm Grateful For ...

My Prayers Today ...

Amen!

Hello God!
Its Me Again

Today I Learned ...

Today I'm Grateful For ...

My Prayers Today ...

Amen!

Hello God!
Its Me Again

Today I Learned ...

Today I'm Grateful For ...

My Prayers Today ...

Amen!

Hello God!
Its Me Again

Today I Learned ...

Today I'm Grateful For ...

My Prayers Today ...

Amen!

Hello God!
Its Me Again

Today I Learned ...

Today I'm Grateful For ...

My Prayers Today ...

Amen!

Hello God!
Its Me Again

Today I Learned …

Today I'm Grateful For …

My Prayers Today …

Amen!

Hello God!
Its Me Again

Today I Learned ...

Today I'm Grateful For ...

My Prayers Today ...

Amen!

Hello God!
Its Me Again

Today I Learned ...

Today I'm Grateful For ...

My Prayers Today ...

Amen!

Hello God!
Its Me Again

Today I Learned ...

Today I'm Grateful For ...

My Prayers Today ...

Amen!

Hello God!
Its Me Again

Today I Learned ...

Today I'm Grateful For ...

My Prayers Today ...

Amen!

Hello God!
Its Me Again

Today I Learned ...

Today I'm Grateful For ...

My Prayers Today ...

Amen!

Hello God!
Its Me Again

Today I Learned ...

Today I'm Grateful For ...

My Prayers Today ...

Amen!

Hello God!
Its Me Again

Today I Learned ...

Today I'm Grateful For ...

My Prayers Today ...

Amen!

Hello God!
Its Me Again

Today I Learned ...

Today I'm Grateful For ...

My Prayers Today ...

Amen!

Hello God!
Its Me Again

Today I Learned ...

Today I'm Grateful For ...

My Prayers Today ...

Amen!

Hello God!
Its Me Again

Today I Learned ...

Today I'm Grateful For ...

My Prayers Today ...

Amen!

Hello God!
Its Me Again

Today I Learned ...

Today I'm Grateful For ...

My Prayers Today ...

Amen!

Hello God!
Its Me Again

Today I Learned ...

Today I'm Grateful For ...

My Prayers Today ...

Amen!

Hello God!
Its Me Again

Today I Learned ...

Today I'm Grateful For ...

My Prayers Today ...

Amen!

Hello God!
Its Me Again

Today I Learned ...

Today I'm Grateful For ...

My Prayers Today ...

Amen!

Hello God!
Its Me Again

Today I Learned ...

Today I'm Grateful For ...

My Prayers Today ...

Amen!

Hello God!
Its Me Again

Today I Learned ...

Today I'm Grateful For ...

My Prayers Today ...

Amen!

Hello God!
Its Me Again

Today I Learned ...

Today I'm Grateful For ...

My Prayers Today ...

Amen!

Hello God!
Its Me Again

Today I Learned ...

Today I'm Grateful For ...

My Prayers Today ...

Amen!

Hello God!
Its Me Again

Today I Learned ...

Today I'm Grateful For ...

My Prayers Today ...

Amen!

Hello God!
Its Me Again

Today I Learned ...

Today I'm Grateful For ...

My Prayers Today ...

Amen!

Hello God!
Its Me Again

Today I Learned ...

Today I'm Grateful For ...

My Prayers Today ...

Amen!

Hello God!
Its Me Again

Today I Learned ...

Today I'm Grateful For ...

My Prayers Today ...

Amen!

Hello God!
Its Me Again

Today I Learned ...

Today I'm Grateful For ...

My Prayers Today ...

Amen!

Hello God!
Its Me Again

Today I Learned ...

Today I'm Grateful For ...

My Prayers Today ...

Amen!

Hello God!
Its Me Again

Today I Learned ...

Today I'm Grateful For ...

My Prayers Today ...

Amen!

Hello God!
Its Me Again

Today I Learned ...

Today I'm Grateful For ...

My Prayers Today ...

Amen!

Made in the USA
Las Vegas, NV
18 January 2022